D0864963

Promise

Promise

poems

SALLY VAN DOREN

Louisiana State University Press
Baton Rouge

Published by Louisiana State University Press
Copyright © 2017 by Sally Van Doren
All rights reserved
Manufactured in the United States of America
LSU Press Paperback Original
First printing

Designer: Michelle A. Neustrom
Typeface: MillerText
Printer and binder: LSI

Poems in this collection were first published as follows: *Cape Rock:* "Me, Myself and I"; *Chariton:* "Bradford Road, around the Back" and "Divided"; *Connecticut River Review:* "Fearless"; *Contemporary American Voices:* "At Least We're Over," "Caesura," "Climbing Out of the Marvelous," "Oracle," "Pit Stop," and "Stoolie"; *December:* "Implausible," "Magician," "Private Practice," "Progress," "What the Sun Says This Cold Morning," "What the Wind Says Before Bed," and "Incentive"; *Diode:* "Expecting Modification"; *Harp and Altar:* "Labor" and "Mimesis"; *Hubbub:* "Color Theory" and "Sfumato"; *The Moth:* "Fallow"; *Pembroke:* "The Book of Usable Minutes"; Poets.org, *Poem-A-Day:* "Call Us" and "Thief"; *Pool:* "For Love to Continue," "House," "Makers," "Anxiety of Influence," "Back to Wendy," "I'm Beat," "Dogs," and "A Woman's Touch"; *Rosebud:* "Housewife as Poet"; *South Carolina Review:* "Or"; *Southern Review:* "What the Moon Says at Sunrise"; *Southwest Review:* "Cahokia"; *Tinge:* "Black Widow"; *2River View:* "Bound," "Defiance," "Justice," and "Monopoly"; *Western Humanities Review:* "Reconciliation."

Library of Congress Cataloging-in-Publication Data

Names: Van Doren, Sally, author.
Title: Promise : poems / Sally Van Doren.
Description: Baton Rouge : Louisiana State University Press, [2017] |
    "LSU Press Paperback Original."
Identifiers: LCCN 2017005128| ISBN 978-0-8071-6691-8 (softcover : acid-
    free paper) | ISBN 978-0-8071-6692-5 (pdf) | ISBN 978-0-8071-6693-2
    (epub) | ISBN 978-0-8071-6694-9 (mobi)
Classification: LCC PS3622.A58548 A6 2017 | DDC 811/.6—dc23
LC record available at https://lccn.loc.gov/2017005128

For Bert

Who kept time with his tail

CONTENTS

PART 2

PART 3

Part 1

Or

Every morning I let it all go.
Then it starts coming back,
sometimes blurred, sometimes
stuttering, sometimes suspended
on a linear dartboard that
I try to impale myself upon.
Even when the skylight is leaking,
I look for the peephole
that will ensnare my vision
of things: the boy sashaying
through the mud, the man shaving,
the mother scrubbing shoes
in the driveway. I want to say
that I feel too, that I remember,
and then I forget, and then I notice
that almost all the leaves are off the trees
and on the ground, save my three magnolias.

Housewife as Poet

I have scrawled audible lifelines along the edges
of the lint trap, dropping the ball of towel fuzz
in the blue bin lined with a thirteen-gallon bag.
My sons' wardrobes lounge on their bedroom floors,
then sidle down to the basement, where I look
forward to the warmth of their waistbands
when I pluck them from the dryer.
Sometimes I wonder why my husband
worries about debt and I wish he wouldn't.
Sometimes I wonder how high the alfalfa
will grow. Sometimes I wonder if the dog
will throw up in the night. Like my mother,
I'm learning not to tamper with anger.
It appears as reliably as the washing machine
thumps and threatens to lurch across the floor
away from the electrical outlet. Nothing's worth
getting worked up about, except for death.
And when I think of the people I have lost,
I wish them back into their button-down shirts,
their raspberry tights.

The Book of Usable Minutes

I heard the mother in the row behind me
explain the safety instructions
to her small noisy children.

I began to calculate how much time
I have spent listening to an automated voice
tell me how to identify the best exit routes,

how to use the seat as a flotation device,
how to place the oxygen mask over my mouth
and continue breathing. If only the flight attendant

could advise me on how to remember
my father, how to say goodbye
to my friend, how not to love my husband.

Climbing Out of the Marvelous

I have learned that knowing a man
is not as easy as it seems.
I have learned that knowing
a woman is even harder.

When I stopped sleepwalking
in concentric reservoirs,
the nurse installed a muzzle
in my chamber pot.

So buoyant was I that no
pipsqueak omen could connive
to smudge my vital gargle. I
camouflaged myself as a warbling hero

and nuzzled up to the organ
in the alcove. Here, kiss-kiss,
our apparent paradigm traipses
to alleviate the superfluous.

We take advantage of the hubbub
and sandwich ourselves under
the hospitable treble clef. We live
for sex or did you know that already?

Monopoly

Trapped in incentive alley
the fuming board game
revised its diffident warehouse
and strutted out into the membrane
ignoring the undercurrents of flame
and adrenaline. The magnet
zipped in its larynx elongated
and with each gulp coins and
jewelry flew to its throat.
With binoculars it was possible
to detect the receding compulsion,
that urge, some might call it,
to climax again and again.
Here, take this tablet if you
can't yet live the allusion.
This goblet's tenured. There's
no mystique about it. If you
check the watermark on the quit deed,
you will know your eyes are dilated
and your personal aquarium
is ready for your morning dip.
The tide is inconsolable.

Me, Myself and I

In the boardroom, bored,
we started analyzing whether
or not the poem was me or I.

The man who wore a cape
dismissed our question
as a callow ruse. He swept

our cognates off the table
and marched to the cafeteria
where he then retracted

his outburst and begged us
to conjugate the plaid tourniquet
we had applied to his throat.

Why did we need *him* to monitor
our atomic mons? We re-
newed ourselves without him.

Cahokia

We plaster the mound
with "has" and "yahs"
making a ruckus so loud
the widows raise the slats
of their blinds to determine
what germ sermons dare side-
step up their ever hallowed grounds,
not the neighboring trash mountain.

We say "boo" and they say
"hush" when they see it's us.
It's a muddy morning and the muck
sticks to our shoes as we circle
and chant, our dreams climbing back
up on the backs of the raindrops.

Expecting Modification

She wants clarity.
She wants precision.

He wants mayhem.
He wants ventilation.

They want a hamburger.
They want rain.

We want repetition.
We want coercion.

You want the unexpected.
You want restoration.

It wants restraint.
It wants the superlative.

I want me.
I want us.

Bradford Road, around the Back

Lovely distortion, here on this deck,
under sun lifting through mist,
a veritable burrow of respite,
where the bobolink, wild turkey
and honeybee entertain
after the arraignment, away from
interrogating eyes. We can hear
here. We can stay here. The gavel
does not fall here. We compose
here, accessories to sex on a picnic table.

Divided

I washed my heart and pinned it
on the clothesline in the basement.
Were I on Bradford Road,
I could hang it outside
between the mudroom door
and the woodshed that is now a deck
equipped with two French lounge chairs
that afford those sitting on them

views to the west and north
of tree masses, parabolas, and
the evergreen drop cloth
that protects Cornwall Hollow
from the blue sky and the white
clouds dripping down upon it.

Finite

The birds learned how to count
to twenty after our phobias about
birth order and astrological signs
subtracted themselves from page one.
We felt we could continue
our quantitative analysis of good
and bad without feeling guilty
about it. I stuck my gullible
wrist into a vat of cellulite
until my mother insisted that I
blowtorch my allegiance to the fat,
fat truth of things. I tried to scrape
off my diligence, but it was as if
a mallet had smashed my binoculars.
I reached for my blindfold in the same
moment that my genealogy gave me
whiplash. My heirloom sat brooding
in the corner of the family room. I filled
in the cigarette burns and played
Chopin's *Prelude*, the curse finally confined
in the quadrant between melody and photosynthesis.

For Love to Continue

It was a humdrum graphite morning.
The subsidiary showed up late
and tired. Her head kept falling
out of its orbit and into
the ventilation queue. When the
astronaut stopped to take off
his makeup, he presented her
with a sachet of primrose
petals in a cracked vitrine.
They entwined themselves on the lattice
only to recoil a bit when an erratic
dilettante usurped their handholds.
With an adroit maneuver, they
sandwiched the euphemism between
his anxiety and her euphoria.
The cordial they squeezed from
their union induced lightheadedness.
They cut out the obit, pasted it
on the last page, then folded the page
in half, folded the corners into triangles
and flicked it across the kitchen table.

Bound

Whoever impeached my son, whoever
punched my son, whoever collapsed
on my son, breaking the brittle
cartoon appliquéd to our front door—
I forgive you. Your rash wheezing, though,
is no substitute for doing the breakfast dishes.
We dawdle at the hospital, eyeing the reclusive
personnel who stalk the emergency room
without name tags. The shrill whistle
of the ambulance metabolizes our
genetic predisposition to nurture. In this vial,
his soul's magma coagulates with the slab
of sentimentality I threw in, hoping it would
thwart the condensation. I threw it in,
unmediated, without the silly man's interference.
It was a risk and now I wait to see if our porcelain iris
will expand or contract. If you would like to join me
on this indistinct stoop, then take the thorn
out of your cleft chin and have a seat.

Labor

Just because the *mouth* houses
Worry doesn't mean that girls
Should act like *flesh* extending
Itself into *terrified nature.*

Our *inert* capacities startle
Even the most educated *bodies.*
Where *dry* meets *cold and naked,*
Breathing always arouses

A crowd and we can *limit*
Our suspicions to the simple
Justice that will carry us further
From *trouble* than our wills.

We *balance inside* on the *slippery,*
Sleeping bed of *hate.*

(Words in italics are taken from Jenny Holzer's *The Living Series,*
1981–1982)

Mimesis

Sasparilla listed her *laments* daily.
The nerve of that *whooping rock*
to *fly* onto her chest moments

after she and Emmett were doing
the right acts with their bodies.
At the edge of transition, *the ceiling*

drizzled *symbols* of sacrifice
that wet her head. When she looked
up she knew she was not *afraid*

to stay on the earth. Her masseuse,
hired by Emmett to rotate her
resilient zygotes, overheard the *spelled*

patterns and began to hunt
down the *father* in the *silver wrapper.*
Sassy's paralysis waned as *the truth*

got *pushed around* in the voting booth.
She dragged Emmett out of the steam
and *licked* his diaphragm. She *carried*

him with her to watch *the facts burn.*
Together they *iced* their blastulae
in the *space* of the *nothing around* them.

(Words in italics are taken from Jenny Holzer's *Laments,* 1987)

Sfumato

I'd like to meet again, not here,
where my adoptives pin me to the walls
of their iconography, not here, in this

fortuitous monastery where I juggle
manic spirals and teeter on the hypotenuse
of simultaneity. We were part of the same

herd, tagged as youths on the Renaissance
Peninsula in a cargo train from Roma
to Siracusa. If we squint, we should be able

to see back far enough to mend our preliminary
misdirection. There, you picked up a charcoal pencil
and sketched a dog in the street. I don't know

where you are now, but I will swear to your
oblique innocence and I promise to show up
this time, at noon at *binario diciannove*.

Reconciliation

As protocols ricochet
from sequence to interval
the convulsive amounts of scope
freeze, making it unlikely

that the sponge will moisten
enough to wipe the contingencies
off the desk. A wanton
contract billows on the top

of the filing cabinet. We tug
at its corners but it rips
in the designated clause
on page three. Our mundane

utilities go unpaid and
the furtive banker seeks
refuge in his calculator.
Time to settle the debt.

At Least We're Over

Yesterday with its gritty
insistence on ruin.
If the sutures holding
all of it together
get snipped, then
the wound reopens
and its discharge
will flood the foyer.

Such drama over
silver polish. Have
our grandmother's
eating utensils become
the instruments of our
last meal at her table?

Color Theory

In May comes the blue window,
but in the meantime, this mean time,
he runs from himself, into glass.

We turned on the flashlight
last night and saw a legless curtain
scurry over a dilated eye.

When it opens again, these anecdotes
will bathe themselves in orange,
ignite and cease to project.

Red is what we really want. Red
in the morning, yellow for lunch
and black at night.

Pit Stop

I became a pilot
because I liked flying
through altitude.

I would pack clouds
in my briefcase
and bring them

home to the kids
on weekends. Once,
en route to Zurich,

I forgot my landing gear.
I developed a fear of telling
stories I could not finish.

Black Widow

I'm going to dismember
your spinnerets.
No more of your orb web
clogging my exoskeleton.
I'll knock that dragline

off its hinge and when
it falls to the ground we
will hear the silk grunt,
the murmur of your venom
dishonored in the dustpan.

I've earned the disposition
of the brown recluse.
My poison's porous, silent.
Hear it swish down your throat
as you take your last breath.

Fearless

In my padded cell
I pat the goose down
walls and look for loose
feathers. It's apparent

that tomorrow might
disgrace me, so I work
backwards and keep my
head affixed to the pillow.

That way no one borrows
my future and no one and I
together confound the sound
of the fall wind. We still have

ears, you see, and though we
are un-fathered, we get up
to plan our succession.

Defiance

We were drawn that way at a young age on the main line
west from St. Louis to the Columbia spur north to Moberly
where our grandparents picked us up at the station

and showed us the quarry behind their house on Gilman Road,
warning us not to try to jump off the edge of the cliff
with an umbrella the way Uncle Robert had.

Our mother had traced our blood to Squire Boone, Daniel's brother.
It coursed through our father's veins when, as a sixteen-year-old
with a summer job on the railroad, he fought to get the cinder

out of the tracks that blocked the switch as the 12:05 bore down on him.
Sixty years later his grandsons spin the wheels of their three speeds
on the gravel path above the wide brown river, sweating

as their knees pump on pedals their feet have out-grown.
We stay at a bed and breakfast on the bluff, walking down
to Dutzow for the Friday night fish fry. Back on our bikes

on the Katy Trail the next morning, stopping along the way
to swing on the vines and poke our heads in the caves,
we race the last mile to the marker in front of the Boone Homestead.

Makers

In a way they led the way for us
his paint brush in her dark room

her pencil on my paper
my watercolor in your gallery

your salary behind my muse
his country house holding your oeuvre

our livelihood swimming under
their gesso, their baby bearing

her ambivalence, our babies bearing
their Michelangelo muscles, you

boring into me, me bearing down on you
our raising, rising, wave-riding, making.

Part 2

Call Us

Let's use our nicknames
when we apply for this next job
even though it's past our bedtime
and our current paycheck

can't shut up the muse
who mewls at the dinner table
begging for a crust of bread
to sate the nightly terrors.

For they come, don't they,
leaving empty spaces numbers
are supposed to fill. Teddy
and Chip loaded their coffers

before the hard freeze.
The ice burns our tongues
as we swallow prosperity
one parched drop at a time.

Blue Surround

Here where gristle disfigures
our vintage placebo. Here

where a clenched double helix
suffocates our fugitive want.

Here where peonies ransack
our right rear flank, where magnolias

popularize our electric loom, where
membranes buzz at touch, where

memories tremor the minute we
jilt them onto a hermetically sealed

moon, there, that one, scalding
our master bedroom window.

The Antithesis of Shy

The syllabus lies next
to the cervix so all one

has to do to master
the material is to seize

the embouchure and pitch
the whole thing forward

into the outskirts of ecstasy
where humming love songs

guarantees parole, where sutures
dissolve like seeds in spring soil.

House

Bedroom

My favorite time
is Friday night
because it takes
the edge off
and I sleep better.

Kitchen

When I'm doing
the dishes he
comes up from
behind and
presses me
into the countertop.
Erotic! I slap him
with the dish towel.

Lawn

He likes to mow
it after lunch
wearing an old
blue work shirt,
shorts and
Carhartt boots.

Deck

We did it once
here last summer

on the picnic table
and I wrote
a poem about
it.

Cellar

Wine bottles, snake skins,
an artificial Christmas
tree that Grandpa
bought that we all
rejected, dirt floor,
wooden stairs.

Guest Room

Mark and Dot in
Colonial portraits
sternly assessing
the needlepoint
sampler across
the room.
"Remembrance is
the sweetest flower
that in a garden grows."

Barn

We have to wear
masks to sweep
out eighty years of
dust, bat shit,

mouse droppings
and dead leaves.

Dining Room

We would like to invite
our old friends to dinner
but she is in rehab
and he is in bed with
the interior decorator.

Living Room

I sit next to the dog and
Wildflowers of North America
avoiding the dark
sooty rectangle
where ashes lie.

Closet

I dare you to open it.

Attainment

It had grown since
the last time. It was
so big I couldn't fit it

in my bloated chasm.
It unlocked my trunk.
It paid my taxes. Like

a torch in blubber it
heated me. We burned
full, fuller, fullest. I flexed

my chest and the culprit came
out and we claimed it right
there in the cul-de-sac.

Implausible

I wanted to take forever
out of the equation and find
out who the man sitting
next to me on the plane was
typing away on his laptop.

I heard him panting
as I ate my warmed almonds,
pistachios and cashews.
We both claimed miscellany
in our bags, but mine held

the benign ingredients
of economic revival. I stowed
them under my seat while
we factored in the happiness
hypothesis. His sadness,

propped up in his glasses case,
secreted a sense of self-worth
tied to a palm tree. I stole
glimpses of his inbox.
We were headed to Miami

after all and we both needed
all the sunscreen we could get.

Progress

The honey crisp apple
fell from the tree
and I took a bite.

I forgot the trend
toward rapture
intoxicated by

the applauding leaves
collapsing from the weight
of their own stems.

In the midst of crow
gossip my teeth
pulverized every last bit

of pulp, core and seeds.
The impertinence of
those lonely branches!

Wheel of Fortune

We get a second chance
to spar with the vacuum
sucking out the dust storm
swirling in our cerebellum.

An astute helicopter
pilot spots amniotic
fluid running from our
nostrils. One kerchoo

and the next generation
fertilizes the ficus tree
shading our most tender
aspirations. If we substitute

a circle for that perpendicular
authoritarian's rules
we will roll along as
we are supposed to.

Empress

Her regime expires when
the moon meets the sun
on the horizon we can't see
because the sycamore trees

next door block our view.
Our world droops in anticipation.
We would like to exchange
the unkind for the kind but

we can't find the strength
to oust the inevitable. Instead
we joke about politics and watch
our neighbors arm themselves.

Justice

The devil trains mother
to train her troubled son
to use a semiautomatic rifle
and he shoots her first

in the face before he opens
fire on the elementary school.
(Father and brother spared,
having long since fled the dirtied

nest.) In his memoirs, the devil cites
as one of his greatest achievements
the introduction of war weapons
as recreational toys in broken

suburban households. That,
and the deprivation of the
rights of a six-year-old
to advance to the second grade.

Magician

Find me a lover
a star to shine
on my dark heart

a light to lighten
the heavy hour
that pulls me forward

into the black box
kicking and screaming
'til his sword halves me.

Chariot

The snow, perplexed, and not
of the caliber we were expecting,
changed its stratagem and

processed upward instead of down.
It chose to embroider
the undersides of the magnolia

leaves with its freckled insignia.
We flipped ourselves over
in response and joined

the drip, drip, drip, landing
in reverse, pooling as we
waited for a ride to the sun.

Four Minutes

Let's hijack this morning
and repair our coincidental

wrongs. You first. Mine
feel too irreversible. In

the interlude I will hire
a genius to barter

for me with the high voltage
powers who turn me on

and off like a kitchen gadget.
How do we pronounce

their names? There's no decorum
anymore on our table top.

Time's up. Please don't degrade
my non sequiturs further.

Two Minutes

You and your
infernal lies!

You and your
blasted reputation!

Crawl right down
to the circle of hell

where you belong
with the hypocrites

and those who
betray their guests!

One Minute

One monolithic minute
interspersed among
migrant profiles

of people we thought
we knew who made
stupendous moves

from one side of our
benevolent mind into
the limbo of the undefined.

Who were you? Under what
obstinate shadow did you hide
yourself? I'm trying to find you

between strokes of this pen,
between these two hands, this
split heart, these last lines.

Two Seconds

I usually eat an apple
around 3:00 every day.

My question is this: how
to respond when it tastes bad?

Stoolie

I have an imaginary lover,
don't you? Fortunately
I see him only when my husband

is away. It's convenient
that he lives across the street
so I can just run right over

after doing the breakfast dishes.
I worry a lot about what
the neighbors will think

if they catch a glimpse of us
on his wrap around porch.
For that reason, we usually

confine our activities to his bathroom
or basement. We couldn't
do anything at my house because

I don't know him well enough
to let him put his head
on my pillow. What if he has

dandruff or one of his nose hairs
were to fall into the sink? My
husband doesn't like finding

hair in the bathroom. My husband
doesn't have much hair on his head
at all. When he comes home, I

stroke his shaved head and smooth
my palms on its nascent bristles.
We dispense with the pillow altogether.

What the Wind Says before Bed

I'm not as superstitious
as you might think.

I pass through the turnstiles
every day without fanfare.

I ration my pleasures
so as not to contaminate

the gray clouds heading
your way. My locomotives

prowl across the plains
in search of you. Do you

flinch when you feel
my hot breath on your neck?

I'm never crooked. I
adjust my motives to my

howling moods. My motto:
Make me whistle. My lullaby:

Rest your head in my maelstrom.

Chaperone

I apprehend his
desire to eavesdrop.

He cringes when I
catch him in the act.

I charge him with
neglect. He took

from us what we
could not protect.

Caesura

And then she stopped, as if
the irritable reaching found
its source, as if the roses were

now painted red, as if each
wayward thought met a new
end, as if drifting did not

lead to calculated hysteria.
She followed her mind, her mouth
and shut down her heart.

Oracle

We've got a knack
for joining routine
cults. Sign here

to make amends
at the intersection
of melody and

mortality. The goat
meat dries on the rack.
We sacrifice what

we don't need and
can afford to kill.
Offer us a pigeon

breast plumped with
harmony and we will
nourish our fear

of flying, or is it
falling? We're fond
of windowpanes and asphalt.

What the Sun Says This Cold Morning

Amscray, Time, you are now
behind me, with your fussbudget

ticking and your neighborly nosiness.
I'm gaining on you every day,

shedding more light on your shady
blunders. Go ahead and subtract

while I add prisms and rainbows.
I'm not caught up in your doorjamb.

I have summoned the locksmith . . .
February opens tomorrow!

What the Moon Says at Sunrise

I'm going away now
but that does not mean
I don't love you.

In fact, I'm quite fond
of your parted lips.
Let me seal them

with mine before I
disappear. Open them
only to eat or to speak.

Give me until sunset
when I will return
to break your promise.

Thief

I remember the hour
you stole time from me

and here in these late pages
I try to collect back

the kisses in the parking lot
that erased my history

next to that green F-150
when you became my future.

Planet

Every once in a while
when I'm spinning out

usually unknowingly
I catch myself against

you, my nipple in your
mouth, back bowed,

hips linked and in
that instant I release

and I'm all over you
and your solid mass.

This Morning's Premise

If I curtsey to your demagogue
will you promise not to detain me

here? I need to move on, past this
erroneous corps of spring pigeons.

How to differentiate between
their yin and our yang?

I want to learn this by heart. How
to walk into the day and claim it.

To the Man Who Drank a Diet Dr. Pepper and a Diet Coke

As I was flying into my third life
I fell asleep and then woke up

my left knee touching his bare leg.
In his earphones, his hair coiled

in a bun on top of his head,
he did not acknowledge my need,

but he permitted it. I thank him now
for not exposing my indiscretion.

Private Practice

My clients are syllables.
I charge them by the consonant.
When there's an ellipsis
I slip them a cheat sheet

and we do deep breathing
until they regain their confidence.
I do pro-bono work
with aspirants. Once I lost

a villanelle to asphyxiation,
but the elegies rallied around
to help me get over it. I'm
having a long term affair

with a sonnet, but it's strictly
confidential. I could be barred
if anyone found out. (I've only
told a limerick or two.) I like

to treat my haiku over sushi
and my ballads with a French
Bordeaux. I work mostly by
referral. With 26 letters out there

I had to add a secretary and a
receptionist just to keep up.
Can't you hear their keyboards?
Tap tap tap, tap tap tap!

Alone and Some

I am missing something.
Papers I did not bring

with me here. The kind
of friends I had where I

came from. My sewing kit.
I cannot even mend your pants.

Fallow

I want so much
as I age even though

I attempt to carve out
a sparse place

for desire. It's as
though a chute opened

last night and there went
all my dreams. I had

nightmares as a result.
I'm sniffling around today

too tired to make sense
of this blue change.

I'm awake now at least, for
as long as I can keep my

eyes open. Maybe I should
do some laundry.

Lay Off

I looked around for you
but I had misplaced
the list of words which

contained your name.
You might prefer that I
delete it from the rolodex

that flips over and over
in my head, replacing one
contact with another every

second or two. I don't rotate
that lightly. While my swivel
chair may have lost the scent

of your patchouli, that bitter funk
lurks right under my nose. I tilt
my head back and twirl in place.

The Kindness of Strangers

Here I am with all my flaws
seeking form and shelter.

I blanche at the notion
of violence, but it's coming

after us, closing in like a
superstition I can't shake.

If I acquiesce to your harsh
future you must promise me

one thing. Where we go we will
find our youth again. Can you

see it there under the yellow linen
tablecloth? I'm depending on it.

Part 3

Anxiety of Influence

My friend, Wendy, no,
she's not anyone you might
have heard of, at least not
a famous poet whose name
I drop all the time (I would
never stoop to such a blatant
expression of insecurity, constantly
projecting through my writing
and art that I run with the right crowd,
all of us desperate for attention,
all of us trying to close off access
to our inner circle) . . . Wendy says
the trick to moving forward is not
to look back.

Back to Wendy

Now that we have established
who she's not, what I really
meant to paraphrase was
her assertion that you, we, one
must not expect to reclaim
a happy past that sits beyond
redemption there over my right
shoulder. Wendy's not
an apologist either. Charge
ahead, she says, with back numbing
syringes that ease the pain
toward an improved
prognosis. We can't say we
know for sure what we will
reproduce. Our systems
falter, our peccadilloes loom
large, our enemies flout
their phonic dominance from
the tops of this megalopolis
built on macadam and market
appeal. Can you recognize
my wrinkled face peering down
at you from the parapet?
I hope so. I've just been
crowned the crone queen.

I'm Beat

When Wendy and I find ten minutes
to write a poem, we do, because we
both know all too well that life
is short when it comes to responding
to cues from the universe. We felt
a rhythm under the pads of our
fingertips on top of the page.
We could have checked on the laundry
or called our accountant, but instead
we bit off more than we can chew,
graphite, ink, erasers, not to mention
lactating and perimenopause and
everything in between. How do
we account for all of this? We can
pause and look back but we can't
really remember what it was like and
tomorrow's demanding in its own way,
even to someone in their fifties, a woman
no less, who has raised a few children.
(When will we be done with that?) Not
yet, we surmise, our own mothers
in their eighties, asking us to get their wool
sweaters from the plastic box under the bed
because they can't get down there themselves.
We bend over. We straighten up. We howl.

Dogs

Wendy is not the person to call
when you are considering
whether or not to put your dog
down. She adores her Havanese
Belle and thinks dogs are a central
component to any effort to achieve
domestic bliss. But our twelve-year-old
Labradoodle Bert has two incurable tumors
and a urinary tract infection. God, he's
a handsome dog, and fit for his years.
But he strains and strains every time
he goes number two which he's
trying to do with increasing frequency.
He's lying on the floor next to me in the sun
quite contentedly now, but we wonder
every morning when we wake up if he
will wake up. Our son lies down on the floor
next to his best friend and I take a picture
of this time of our lives coming to an end.

Bert

Of course it turns out Wendy
is exactly the person to call
when you lose your dog because
she believes that he will live on
in our family lore, as does
their ferret Folly who so many
years ago was squooshed
in the swing door between
their kitchen and dining room.

Incentive

I'm considering dumping Wendy
for Etel, who gives me more

concrete directions to the sea
and sky, but I've been betrayed

before (haven't you?) and I know
how it feels to look back for your

friend and see no one staring you
in the face. I'll invite Wendy to tour

the botanical garden with me and there
maybe we can migrate from the redbuds

to the dogwoods as though nature
has known all along what it was doing.

A Woman's Touch

If you don't mind, I would
like to invite Wendy into the
conversation one more time
mostly since we appear to be
sitting on a fulcrum between
the before and the after and I
don't want to be accused of
kvetching all by my lonesome.
Wendy's moniker is a mono-
chromatic needlepoint crest
symptomatic of an only child
who is subconsciously linked
genetically to my anthems.
She takes one stitch at a time
and calibrates the threat of
tomorrow next to today's
disappointment. You'll find
the difference incremental,
but the pigments she chooses
to depict the morning light
in late May . . . these are unsurpassed.
So we sit in our comfy chair
and ransom ourselves to the future.

This or That

Please tell me we can stop
consulting Wendy about

every "momentous" moment
we encounter. And since when

did we become plural? Last night
when our feathers were ruffled

by the stranger who flew
in the window to accost us.

We're not accustomed to con-
tentiousness. We're used

to dear sweet Wendy who
knows exactly what we've lost.

3D

You might be pleased
to know that just a few
days ago I procured

Wendy's permission to go
public, as it were, with her
very private utterances.

Belle, too, acquiesced, but at no
ruffle to her plush coat. My
freedom, though, comes

at a price. I would like, for once,
to call a truce with the force
that pushes me out while

at the same time pulls me in.
Where to hide? I think I'll drag
Wendy out to the horizon with me.

From that flat line we for sure
will be able to determine
where she ends and I begin.

NOTES

The title "Housewife as Poet" owes a debt to Elisabeth Eybers' poem "Poet as Housewife."

The title "The Book of Usable Minutes" is taken from a line in John Ashbery's poem "Train Rising Out of the Sea."

The title "Climbing Out of the Marvelous" owes a debt to Seamus Heaney's poem "Lightenings."

The title "Blue Surround" is taken from the title of a Richard Diebenkorn print.

"The Kindness of Strangers" draws its title and several other words and phrases from Tennessee Williams' play *A Streetcar Named Desire*.

CPSIA information can be obtained
at www.ICGtesting.com
Printed in the USA
LVOW11s0251100817
544485LV00001B/111/P